1

HOW TO START & GROW A BUSINESS

A concise guide on how to start both small / large businesses, pros and cons, what's needed and structures to put in place

Davis G. Malcom
Ph.D.

Table of Content

Introduction

Mindset

What is it that you assume you really must have to construct a fruitful startup? Obviously, you need a good idea and a plan of action that works, however it is likewise imperative to have the right mindset. You want to have both a positive and a growth mindset to ensure your business succeeds. However, not every person gets results. Some don't have the drive to drive themselves to where they

*should be to succeed. I'll share with you
why the right mindset,
entrepreneurship, and business are
closely connected.*

A Growth and Abundance Mindset

*Numerous business people think they
understand what they're doing. Yet, in
the event that they don't have a Growth
mindset and mentality, they may very
well won't ever learn. Without
information available, you can't plan,
test or execute the right methodology.
Assuming that you lack confidence in
yourself, your startup will probably
fizzle.*

Many hopeful business visionaries (entrepreneurs) have a growth and abundance mindset yet they lack the hunger and drive to push themselves to follow up on it. It's extremely simple to become familiar with what you're doing assuming it's made you money previously. In any case, this is the most exceedingly terrible method for starting or maintaining a business. A startup needs development and innovation to be successful.

In particular, fostering a growth mindset can keep you from procrastination. I've seen numerous entrepreneurs sit around staring in light of the fact that they don't have a growth mindset. Rather than making a move, they lounge around contemplating what they ought to or shouldn't do. This is in many cases a significant mistake and burns a huge measure of time.

To foster a growth mentality, you should recognize your reasons behind you doing that business. Come at the situation from your client's perspective. What might satisfy them assuming you tackled their concern? Assuming that you know the response, you will be more propelled to take care of issues.

Whenever you have distinguished your justification for being good to go, record that reason and keep on considering it consistently. Continue to keep in mind why you decided to begin this sort of business in the first place.

The response to that question will assist you with sorting out a way to steer your startup in the correct direction.

A Positive Mindset

A positive outlook is powered by self-confidence and a healthy mental self-view. When you have a major sense of self-esteem, you can set your whole self in motion. A solid healthy mental self-worth and confidence can assist you with paying attention to your instinct and taking the plunge in any event, even if hard times arise.

By setting your whole self in motion, you can make a strong force to move you forward with your startup. Have a go at posing a significant inquiry: "What is preventing me from succeeding in my startup?" As you consider it, the response ought to be clear to you.

I began focusing on this thought toward the start of 2015. I tested myself on whether I had the right mentality to drive myself to pull through all the stops. Furthermore, I started to second guess myself on that theme. I would challenge myself one day and drive myself further the following day. The key is to keep on making it happen.

The right mindset is an amazing asset. It permits you to take full advantage of every available open door or opportunity. In the event that you are not using this asset to its maximum capacity or full potential, you are burning through your time. Keep in mind, life is short, so exploit consistently every second you have. Drive yourself to get what you need, then, at that point, take in the scenery!

Chapter 1

An Entrepreneur

There is more to being a successful entrepreneur than just starting new businesses every other day. It implies the right demeanor or attitude towards a business and the assurance and coarseness to make progress.

A fruitful business person has areas of strength for a drive that helps that person to succeed. Allow us to investigate the characteristics that go into making an effective and successful entrepreneur.

The prospect of work should excite an entrepreneur. They ought to continuously have major areas of strength for you to succeed and conquer hindrances. Not only should they set ambitious goals for themselves, but they should also demonstrate that they are actually committed to achieving them despite the numerous obstacles they face.

A fruitful or determined entrepreneur generally has serious areas of strength of fearlessness and a healthy opinion of their abilities, skills, and capacities. Their character and personality is strong and solid. They are constantly engaged and don't actually dither with the little things in need of attention.

They stand out from the rest because of this.

An entrepreneur ought to constantly be keeping watch for new developments, innovations, and better ideas to always rise as a winner. They should constantly reinvent themselves, come up with better business strategies, and improvise on the goods and services they provide. One more significant nature of a fruitful business person is receptiveness in taking on change. They ought not to be hardheaded and obstinate with regards to picking different choices. Change is the main thing that is consistent in business because nobody can consistently create any gains on age old strategies.

The way to progress lies in development or evolution, whether it is advancement of ideas, goods and services, technology. An Entrepreneur ought to have a receptive mindset, energy and excitement to learn new things. It is basic to comprehend that the best way to keep being at the top is to continue to change and evolve with the time.

A business person or entrepreneur ought to know about the most recent service techniques and technology to serve the clients in a superior manner.

Rivalry and competition ought to never startle an entrepreneur. Competition is what a fruitful business visionary blossoms with, as a matter of fact. Restraining infrastructure is never

something worth being thankful for.
This is on the grounds that in imposing
a business model there is no extension
for impromptu creation or change.

A business person ought to be
exceptionally vivacious and persuaded.
The individual in question ought to
continuously be on the go.
Simultaneously, the responsibility levels
must be high. Just when an individual
is persuaded or motivated might he at
any point do justice to his work?

Tolerating rejection or productive
analysis can go far in making a
business person successful. Analysis
shows what the person isn't doing as
expected or where change is required.
Nonetheless, it should be recalled that

tolerant analysis is a vital approach to getting achievement.

This is on the grounds that an individual will then, at that point, know about the deficiencies of his business and as needs be set things right. Consequently tolerating analysis is really a decent approach to improvising.

Energy, resourcefulness, readiness to make do and pay attention to other people and serious determination to succeed makes an entrepreneur effective. Furthermore, this is the very thing you need to remember too if you have any desire to be a successful entrepreneur yourself.

The Lifestyle of a Successful Entrepreneur

Entrepreneurs have more control over their day to day schedule and can seek after their desired work. While this lifestyle sounds marvelous alongside the automated revenue that goes along the way, it takes a great deal of difficult work and discipline to reach and keep up with that level.

Entrepreneurs apply viable and effective habits to make progress and make a positive impact in their communities.

Knowing the Lifestyle of an effective and successful entrepreneur can assist you with growing an energetic business and improve your efficiency.

How does a successful entrepreneur live their life? The existence of a successful entrepreneur spins around day to day improvements, schedules, and mindset shifts that permit us to perform at a significant level.

Here are a few Habits and Lifestyle:

1. Set Clear Objectives and Goals

Setting clear objectives makes it more straightforward and easier to follow your headway and make a move on your business. The clearness in this aspect can direct your endeavors and keep you zeroed in on what fundamentally affects your organization's income. You can set goals and objectives around production targets, income achievements, and other quantifiable objectives. Entrepreneurs can likewise set deadlines for providing key expectations.

2. Focus on Physical, Mental and Emotional Health

A successful entrepreneur's lifestyle includes more than just hard work on a business. Entrepreneurs additionally focus on their physical and psychological health. These people exercise on different occasions every week and get sufficient sleep every night. To improve their mental health, entrepreneurs engage in practices like journaling and meditation.

3. Maintain discipline

Entrepreneurs have the control wheel. While this gives a great deal of opportunity and adaptability, you likewise need to be over everything. You don't have a supervisor instructing you to return to work. It depends on you to keep grinding and working on what makes the biggest difference for your business. The lifestyle of an entrepreneur spins around consistent discipline. You can set alarms and reminders on your phone that propel you to return to work and check out at your objectives and goals consistently.

4. Open to Changes

The world moves quickly, and it can feel faster for a business person who shuffles numerous business decisions in an evolving market. A great entrepreneur figures out how to adjust in light of changes in the work environment, client conduct, macroeconomic circumstances, and different variables. An entrepreneur can grow and become a better leader by being open to change.

5. Communicate Effectively

Entrepreneurs keep up with compelling and good communication with their workers and staff. Whenever the organization gets bigger, entrepreneurs hire what we call "point of contact" who speak with staff and hand-off their messages to the entrepreneurs. The achievement or disappointment of any business is somewhat influenced by how rapidly information goes all through the organization and the accuracy of the information.

6. Calculate Risk and Risk Management

Entering a business requires risk-taking. A successful entrepreneur's lifestyle includes taking calculated risks. On the off chance that an entrepreneur needs more clients, they must decide if it's a good idea to purchase a second retail store, put more cash into internet publicizing (advertisement) or double the social media and entertainment promoting endeavors. Every one of these decisions may cost time and cash. Entrepreneurs take a careful study on data and information to survey which decision provides them with the most noteworthy probability of progress and the most ideal result.

7. Keep a Healthy Balance between Work and fun activities

Business people are diligent and hard workers, yet they likewise know when to step away. They invest time with their families and work on their leisure activities. Enjoying breaks permits business people to get back to work feeling prepared to handle new difficulties. The re-charge can likewise assist with efficiency. Planning seven days' vacation and making yourself accessible to loved ones at night can assist you with keeping a sound balance between work and fun activities.

8. Take care of Issues Proactively

Business people follow up on an issue as opposed to standing by inactively for a conclusion. In order to keep talented employees and maintain positive customer relationships, business owners must actively resolve conflicts.

9. More Efficiently With Less Work

Business people lack the ability to deal with talking endlessly in work spaces. Full-time workers optimize their time so they can seek after their business projects during lunch hours and later in the day. These people begin working early and finish their key errands

*sooner than others. They limit likely
interruptions, and some of them get up
in the early morning to begin.
Entrepreneurs don't really work longer
than every other person, yet they are
effective, proficient and understand
what should be done.*

*10. Think about Disappointments and
Failures as a valuable learning
opportunity.*

*No one's perfect, however the manner
in which individuals view those errors
can prompt upgrades and
improvement. As a result of constantly
experimenting with new business
concepts and projects, entrepreneurs
frequently make numerous mistakes.
Rather than getting deterred by their
mistakes, entrepreneurs view them as*

learning opportunities. They endeavor to turn out to be better with every disappointment and use those mistakes as illustrations to build successful organizations.

11. Observe Little Wins

Entrepreneurs often set ambitious goals and objectives, yet they additionally know how to celebrate little wins. Enjoying little breaks to recognize little wins can spur you to go after greater goals and objectives and set forth more effort. In the event that you just glance at large milestones and spotlight on how far you are away from them that can become deterring and discouraging. However, celebrating these little wins assists entrepreneurs with strong momentum and energy to accomplish greater successes later on.

12. Manage Funds and Finances Responsibly

Each and every successful entrepreneur has a steady head over their funds. A decent plan of action with a constant flow of clients can in any case implode or collapse on the off chance that the funds and finances aren't maintained, managed or controlled. Tracking income and expenses is a crucial part of a successful entrepreneur's lifestyle. You can record your expenses, and take a look at your past ledger and financial records to calculate how you use your cash.

13. Welcome Competition

Successful Entrepreneurs are not terrified of competition because it empowers cooperation opportunities and moves entrepreneurs to work on their art. Entrepreneurs who work from a condition of dread and fear don't remain or last for a really long time.

14. Allow others to be Leaders

Entrepreneurs are leaders and go with choices all alone, yet you should likewise offer your workers chances to lead and decide. Assuming an organization depends on an entrepreneur for decisions and key choices, that business person will battle to go on get-away and vacations.

Permitting others to lead at some point guarantees the organization can run as expected even without you. Showing you have a decent, skilled and good team can likewise help you with demanding a higher value when you one day want to sell your organization.

15. Value Networking

Entrepreneurs connect and associate with different entrepreneurs in the industry to build their network. An enormous Network gives an entrepreneur more assets and easier market to specific business sectors and opportunity. You can associate with 1-5 individuals every day on informal networks like LinkedIn and by chatting with entrepreneurs in your neighborhood local area.

16. Embrace long lasting Learning

Consistently learn new things by understanding books, paying attention to digital recordings, and consuming other data. They concentrate on the center parts, like business illustrations and self-awareness, yet they additionally see market patterns and what's going on in the economy.

17. Certain and comfortable

Entrepreneurs are more than a little flawed and commit numerous errors, yet they are positive about their choices and confident on their decisions. A choice carried out with certainty can get a business person farther than making a similar move while lacking certainty.

Entrepreneurs can gain from their mistakes, adjust, and pay attention to feedback, however certainty is a vital part of business ventures.

Setting out on the Entrepreneurial Journey

The lifestyle of an entrepreneur can be very rewarding! Entrepreneurs get to settle on choices for their organizations, employees, pursue the career they love, and new clients.

Chapter 2

Seeing Yourself as an Entrepreneur

Beginning a business is a cycle that requires a great measure of thought and cautious assessment. To begin with, you really want to look hard and long at your assets, skills and abilities, and of course weaknesses. This will permit you to begin pondering what you can do and what you can't do. It is vital to begin here regardless of whether you as of now have the world's best business idea, but you probably won't have what it takes or character qualities to empower you to make a successful business. You want to come up with business concepts where you naturally have the greatest potential for success, like: An individual with a good degree of programming expertise is very much suited to beginning a web programming company or agency. If you have a short attention span, you might not want to think about businesses that deal with accounting. A man that is naive and too reserved or doesn't like addressing new individuals wouldn't consider a vigorous client confronting business. These are only three general examples, yet it provides you with an inkling. The significant point is to figure out yourself and your team (if you have any at all) and assume you are appropriate to any business ideas, areas of business or types of business. It permits you to come up with good ideas and narrows down what businesses you could begin with.

Find Your Motivation for starting the Business

Before you start a business, you ought to be totally clear about why you are making it happen. That might sound self-evident, yet there are really many justifications and reasons for why somebody will just decide to leave the security that a job and career provides for the uncertainty of starting a new business. So the more clearly you are about precisely what you are trying to accomplish, the better opportunity you have of accomplishing it.

Fame, Power, Influence, Wealth, Saving the world?

Many entrepreneurs are persuaded, inspired or motivated by a blend of the abovementioned albeit most don't want to just let it out and admit it.

Understanding what is driving you to start a business is a main consideration in figuring out what kind of business you ought to start. Why? It's because when a business you start isn't lined up with individual desire, personal goals and ambitions, it is significantly more likely you will fail at it. You ought to ensure from the outset that your own objectives, goals and drive are viable or

compatible with your business, for
instance:

i. Somebody who is out for Wealth
should take a look at organizations in
the monetary/financial service
industry, where Fintech valuations and
incomes are normally a lot higher than
other start-up businesses or companies.
Somebody who looks for power and
impact could accomplish this through
any type of media business.

ii. Somebody who is out for influence,
control and power may be the most
ideal to any form of media business.

iii. Somebody who needs to save the
world could begin a business handling
environmental change through
renewable energy or power. It is

essential to comprehend the reason why you are beginning a business so you can zero in on business thoughts that will assist you with getting to where you need to go.

Ensure It's A Valid justification To Start

In view of reality, you probably won't start a business for just one reason; rather, it will probably be a combination of several of them. So know that the aims might struggle or conflict with one another. Making a long-run family company to pass down the ages, for instance, likely could be contrary to making a serious fortune, since you might find out at a certain *point that you really want to sell the business to understand its full worth.*

While it is feasible to make a successful business exclusively to rake in boatloads of cash, as a general rule, it will be difficult work in the event that there isn't undoubtedly another component acting as an inspiration. This is on the grounds that it can require numerous years between starting a business and getting any interest or money from it - if ever - and the difficult work required is monstrous, and the chance of disappointment and failure is very real.

Essentially putting your faith or hopes in a future conceivable treasure is probably not going to be sufficient to support you through the troublesome times. So ensure you have a valid justification, try sincerely and take it all in!

Grasp and Understand Your Entrepreneurial Passion

With regards to starting a business, in the event that you are energetic about it, you will be bound to find a lasting success. The primary justification for this is straightforward: that is you will work harder and persevere more on a business you are energetic and passionate about, consequently be bound to prevail at it. Passion is frequently the only factor that distinguishes successful entrepreneurs from unsuccessful ones.

That's what rationale or logic directs in the event that you need a successful business, you ought to start in a space that you have an enthusiasm and passion for. To begin sorting out what business or areas of business you are or could be enthusiastic about, start by thinking about the areas, activities and things you are passionate about, that is to say, that interest you and you have sincere feelings on, for instance: Someone who enjoys hiking might want to start a travel company. Somebody who loves Lego could ponder a toy or development business. Somebody who all through his or her life has a passion for music could start a company related to sound. While considering offline or online business ideas remember that beginning any business is adequately hard, assuming you ensure it is one you

are enthusiastic about you are
significantly more prone to succeed.

Chapter 3

Coming Up With Great Business Ideas/Research Your Business Ideas

Concocting a business idea is somewhat simple, thinking of an extraordinary business idea is hard. It is basic and important to your success that when starting, you research and explore different ideas before deciding on the one you will get on with

Most business guidance advises you to adapt what you love, yet it misses two *other vital components: it should be productive and something you're great at. For instance, you might love music, yet how reasonable is your business idea in the event that you're not an extraordinary vocalist or lyricist? Perhaps you love making soap and need to open a shop in your unassuming community that as of now has three shops nearby — it will not be easy to corner the market while you're making similar items as others around there.*

In the event that you don't have a firm idea of what your business will involve, ask yourself these:

- ☐ *What do you very much love to do?*
- ☐ *What do you despise doing?*

- ☐ *Can you at any point think of something that could make those things much easier?*
- ☐ *What are you great at?*
- ☐ *What do others come to you for guidance about?*
- ☐ *In the event that you were given ten minutes to allow a five-minute discourse on any topic, what might it be?*

These inquiries can lead you to an idea for your business.

Assuming you have a business idea, these questions could assist you with growing it. When you have your idea, measure it against whether you're great at it and assuming it's productive and profitable.

Your business thought additionally doesn't need to be the following Scour Daddy or Squatty Patty. All things considered, you can take an existing item and develop it. You can likewise sell a digital product.

What Sort of Business Would it be a good idea for you to start?

Before you pick the kind of business to begin, there are a critical interesting points:

- *What sort of funding do you have?*
- *How long do you need to put resources into your business?*

- *Do you like to work from an office, or a workshop, or from home?*
- *What passion and interests do you have?*
- *Could you at any point sell information (like a course), instead of an item?*
- *What abilities and skill sets do you have?*
- *How quick do you need to scale your business?*
- *What sort of help and support do you need to begin your business?*
- *Are you banding together with another person? Like partnership?*
- *Does the establishment model sound good to you?*

Another Method of Generating Business Ideas.

This phase is in many cases a long and tedious cycle however have some persistence and you will rejuvenate a few fabulous ones. Below you will find guidance on the most proficient method to get everything rolling in the ideation cycle and concoct extraordinary business ideas.

1. Tackle A Problem That Clients and Customers Care About

Begin by contemplating what huge issues you could tackle and how. Numerous effective and successful organizations began to take care of genuine issues that influence a huge number of individuals and give an answer through their products, goods and services.

For instance, Tesla began with the target of making the vehicles purely electric and they are well on the way having built a multi-million dollar business all the while.

2. Identify Where You Give A Better Solution

Search for regions where solutions are now accessible however you can show improvement and do better than already existing businesses, organizations or companies either with respect to innovations, advancement, efficiency or cost.

For instance, Apple entered the phone market over 10 years ago as an underdog with another creative product and are now currently a market leader. In spite of the reality that the technology had been accessible for quite a long time nobody had brought the degree of development that iPhone did to the market.

3. Be less expensive Than Others

You ought to search for areas where you can give critical savings to the client and customers versus competition. These kinds of businesses become unbelievably quick, especially during downturns and recession.

For instance, Poundland is an extraordinary illustration of this sort of business, since its initiation of its pre-owned cost as the essential differentiator to its rivals. Through offering the most reduced cost/ lowest price possible on a major scope of consumer product, the business has developed to an exceptionally effective high road chain.

4. Develop In a Conventional Slow Changing Market

Is there a field of business or industry that hasn't seen a lot of development in the last 10-100 years? This is much of the time the case in non-tech enterprises that are slow to push forward change while the state of affairs stays beneficial.

*5. Try not to Restrict Yourself to One
Business Idea*

*It is not difficult to choose one idea, yet
to allow yourself the best opportunity of
thinking of an extraordinary idea, it's
ideal to pick a couple to look at.*

*6. Assuming You're Stuck, Stop
Thinking*

*You can overthink it with regards to
ideation, so assuming you are stuck,
quit mulling over everything.
Commonly, when you stop overthinking
something the idea or Solution will
come to you later.*

*7. Construct a Business for a Future
Need or Market*

*Attempt to think into the future, what
will the world resemble in 5 or 10
years? Contemplating the future will
permit you to think about new business
sectors and markets that might open
because of developments, technology, or
innovations.*

*For instance, cryptocurrencies like
Bitcoin over the most recent couple of
years have become huge business
sectors without anyone else with an
entire ecosystem of infrastructure and
technology suppliers developing around
it.*

8. Copy Similar Businesses and Be Better

It is very unlikely, except if you are on the bleeding edge of technology, that your business ideas are different or say unique. A lot of the world's greatest organizations were not progressive or revolutionary, at this point they came into the market with very developed players and just beat every other business.

You must not have the most unique Plan to make a splendid business, you simply need to show improvement over any other person! For instance, Microsoft appeared unexpectedly and beat each and every contender to turn into the prevailing operating system supplier in the mid 1990's.

9. Transform Your Hobby into A Business

A legitimate leap is to take a hobby and transform it into an ideal business. Why? A hobby is something you definitely know a ton about, obviously have a passion for and you will know where to begin. For instance, it is intelligent to go from collecting models to selling models.

10. Think about a Global Business

The world is presently an exceptionally worldwide spot, you can have a business in China and work it from New Zealand assuming that that is what you want. Globalization and technology offer huge potential outcomes to run business in new and developing markets all over the world.

In the event that the circumstances are not ideal for your plan of action in your home country market, search for a country where they are. For instance, Rocket internet fabricated their multi-million dollar business by copying inventive plans of action from developed markets or Business and taking them to less-less markets where they were the only company.

11. Research Your Business Ideas

This stage is tied in with exploring your business ideas as much as possible to decide if your ideas could transform into an extraordinary business. To survey and compare each, you need to have a reasonable comprehension of the points below.

12. Characterize and Examine Your Target Market

Is there a market for the product and services, or business? And is it sufficiently large to help your objectives and goals? You ought to likewise think about the serious scene and know who your fundamental competitors are. Examine what their and your weaknesses and strengths are, as well as market potential opportunities and threats. You need a reasonable thought of the general market and how your business would squeeze into it.

13. Check whether there's a demand For Goods and Services

Is there an immediate demand for your merchandise or will you need to educate clients or customers about the requirement for your product or services?

14. Grasp and understand your potential clients

You ought to have an unmistakable idea of who your potential clients and customers are, including business details, demographic information or data etc. in the event that you are selling B2B.

*Have A Business Plan That Checks out
(although I will talk about this in the
next chapter)*

*Having a good comprehension of how
you would reach your potential
customers in order to grow and develop
your market is basic to succeed. In
particular, understanding what sales
and marketing channels you will need
to go after and how.*

Research Your Rivals and Market

*Most entrepreneurs invest more energy
on their products than they do getting
to know the competition. In the event
that you at any point apply for outside
funding, the lender wants to know or*

*the accomplice needs to be aware: what
makes you (or your business idea)
unique? In the event that market
examination and analysis shows your
products and services are saturated in
your region or area, try to think of a
different methodology or approach.
Take housekeeping, for instance — as
opposed to general cleaning services,
you could have some expertise in homes
with pets or just on garage cleanups.*

Essential Exploration (Primary Research)

*The main phase of any competition
study is primary research, which
involves getting information directly
from potential clients as opposed to
putting together your conclusions and*

decisions with mere assumptions. You can use interviews, questionnaires, or surveys to know what these consumers need.

Studying loved ones, I mean family and friends isn't suggested except if they're your objective or target market. Individuals who say they'd purchase something and individuals who really do purchase it are really different. The last thing you need is to put such a lot of confidence in what they say, make the product and fail when you attempt to sell it since each individual who said they'd get it won't, because the item isn't something they wanted to purchase.

Auxiliary Exploration (Secondary Research)

Use existing sources of data, like census information, to assemble data when you do secondary research. The current information might be contemplated, accumulated and analyzed in different ways that are fitting for your requirements however it may not be as definite and concise as essential exploration (primary research).

Conduct a SWOT Analysis

SWOT represents strengths, weaknesses, opportunities and threats. Conducting a SWOT examination permits you to take a look at current realities about how your goods, services or ideas could perform whenever taken to market, and it can likewise assist you with coming to conclusions about the direction of your ideas. Your business ideas could have a few errors that you hadn't thought of or there might be a few chances to make an improvement on a competitor's product.

Chapter 4

Create a Business Plan

A business plan and strategy is a unique document that fills in as a guide for laying out a new business. Potential investors, financial institutions, and company management are the ones these documents are made for. Regardless of whether you decide to self-finance your business, a business plan and strategy can assist you with fully exploring your Ideas and spot possible issues or errors. **Include the following sections when writing a comprehensive business plan:**

Executive outline and Summary:
The executive summary ought to be the primary thing in the business plan, however it ought to be written last. It depicts the proposed new business and features the objectives or goals of the company, business or organization and the techniques or steps to accomplish them.

Organization, business or Company description: *The Business description covers what issues your goods, services or product addresses and why your business or idea is unique. For instance, perhaps your experience is in molecular engineering, and you've used that foundation to make another type of athletic wear —*

you have the appropriate qualifications to make the best material.

Market analysis: *This part of the business plan looks at a company's position in relation to its competitors. The market analysis ought to incorporate target market, market size, segmentation analysis, development rate, patterns and a competitive climate evaluation.*

Association and structures: *Write on the kind of business organization you want, what risk the board of management, and who will staff the management crew. What qualifications do they have? Will your business be a single-member limited liability company (LLC) or a corporation?*

***Mission, Goals, and objectives**: This part ought to contain a concise statement of purpose and detail what the business wishes to achieve and the moves toward getting there. These objectives ought to be SMART (specific, measurable, action-orientated, realistic and time-bound).*

***Products or Services**: This segment portrays how your business will work. It includes the products that you will sell to customers when your company first starts, how they compare to those of your competitors, how much they cost, who will be in charge of making the products, how you will get materials, and how much it will cost to make them.*

73

Background summary: *The writing of this section of the business plan takes most of the time. Arrange and sum up any information, articles and research contents that concentrate on patterns that could negatively or positively influence your business or industry.*

Marketing plan: *The marketing plan identifies the characteristics of your products, goods or Services, sums up the SWOT analysis and also examines competitors. It additionally analyses how you'll advance your business, how much cash will be spent on marketing and advertising and how lengthy the campaign is supposed to be.*

Plan for finances: *The financial plan is probably the most important part of the business plan because the company* can't move forward without money. Be sure to include a proposed spending plan (budget) in your financial plan alongside financial statements, for example, a balance sheet, income statement and statement of cash flow. Generally, five years of projected budget reports are adequate. This part is additionally where you ought to include your financial request in the event that you're going for outside funding.

An exit Strategy: An exit strategy is significant for any business that is looking for financing since it frames how you'll sell the organization or move proprietorship assuming you choose to resign or continue on toward different projects. When it comes time to sell your business, you can also get the most *value out of it with an exit strategy. There are maybe a couple choices for exiting a business, and the most ideal choice for you relies upon your objectives, goals, circumstances and conditions.*

The most widely recognized exit strategy are:

Shutting the doors and leaving Selling the business to another party Transferring the business to members of one's family Selling the business resources and assets.

Develop a Scalable Business Model

As your business grows and develops more, it's vital to have a Scalable Business Model so you can accommodate extra clients and customers without incurring extra expenses. A Scalable Business Model is one that can be recreated easily to serve more clients without a huge expansion in costs.

<u>Here are few usual scalable Business Model</u>:

- ✓ *Franchise Company or Business*
- ✓ *Business, organization, company (etc.) that sell digital goods or product*

- ✓ Subscription-based company or business
- ✓ Network marketing organizations

Plan Your Taxes

One of the main things to do while beginning a business, organization or company is to begin planning to pay taxes. Taxes can be mind boggling and complicated and there are a few distinct kinds of taxes you might be responsible for, including property tax, income tax, sales tax and employment tax. Contingent upon the sort of business you're working, you may likewise be expected to pay different taxes, for example, unemployment tax.

Pick Your Business structure

While organizing or structuring your business, it's fundamental to consider what each structure means for how much tax you owe, day to day tasks and whether your own resources are in danger.

LLC

An LLC limits your risk for business debts. LLCs can be owned by at least one individual, set of individuals, or organizations and should incorporate a registered agent. These owners are alluded to as members.

Pros

LLCs shield owners from personal liability.
They're one of the simplest business entities to set up. You can have a single-member LLC

Cons

You might be expected to record extra desk work with your state consistently
LLCs can't give stock
You'll have to pay yearly documenting charges to your state.

Limited Liability Partnership (LLP)

Similar to an LLC, an LLP is typically used by licensed business professionals like accountants and attorneys. These plans require a partnership agreement.

Pros

Partners are only partially liable for the LLP's debts and actions.
LLPs are not difficult to form and don't need a lot of desk work
An LLP can have as many partners as it wants.

Cons

Partners are expected to partake in the business effectively

LLPs can't give stock
All partners are actually at risk for any
malpractice claims against the
business.

Sole Ownership

On the off chance that you start a solo
business, you should seriously consider
sole ownership. The organization and
the owner, for lawful and tax reasons,
are seen the same. The owner of the
business is responsible for the company.
Thus, assuming the business falls flat,
the owner is monetarily and personally
liable for all business debts if there be
any.

Pros

Sole ownerships are not difficult to form
There's no need or reason to record extra paperwork work with your state
The company is completely under your control.

Cons

You're by and by responsible for all business debts Fund-raising for a sole proprietorship can be troublesome
The business might have a restricted or limited life span.

Chapter 5

Register Your Business and Get Licenses

There are a few lawful issues to address while beginning a business subsequent to picking the business structure. Coming up next is a decent agenda of things to consider while laying out your business:

Pick Your Business Name

Make it memorable and vital yet not excessively difficult. Pick a similar domain name, if available, to lay out your internet presence. A business name can't be the same with organization, Business, company or agency in your state, nor might it at any point encroach on another brand name or trademark that is as of now enrolled and registered with the US Patent and Trademark Office (USPTO).

Business Name versus DBA

There are business names, and afterward there are made up business names referred to as "Doing Business As" or DBA. You might have to document a DBA in the event that you're working under a name that is not quite the same as the legitimate name of your business. For instance, "Mike's Bicycle Shop" is doing business as "Mike's Bicycles." The legitimate name of the business is "Mike's Bicycle Shop," and "Mike's Bicycles" is the DBA.

You might have to record a DBA with your state, region or regional government offices. ***The advantages of a DBA include:***

- ○ *It can assist you with starting a business Bank account under your business name*
- ○ *A DBA can be utilized as a "trademark" to mark or trade your products, goods or services.*
- ○ *A DBA can be used to get a permit to operate*

Register Your Business and Get an EIN

You'll formally create a corporation, LLC or other business entities by filling in document forms with your state's business agency—usually the Secretary of State. As a part of this whole process, you'll have to pick an enrolled or registered agent to account for and accept any legal doc for your business. You'll likewise pay a filling expense. The state will send you a certificate that you can use to apply for licenses, a Tax Identification Number (TIN) and business bank acc.

Then, apply for an EIN (employer identification number)
All businesses, companies, organizations, other than sole

proprietorship without employees, should and must have a government business employer identification number. Present your application to the IRS and you'll receive your number in minutes.

Get Proper Licenses and Allows

Legitimate requirements are overseen and determined by your industry and ward or jurisdiction. Most organizations need a combination of local, state and federal license to work. Check with your local government office (and, surprisingly, a lawyer) for licensing data information and Data custom-made to your area.

Set Your Funds and Finances in Order

1. Open a Business Bank Account

Keep your business and individual finances very separate. This is the way to pick a business financial records — and why separate business accounts are fundamental. At the point when you open a business account, you'll have to give your business name and your business Tax Identification Number (EIN). This business account can be used for your deals, like paying your supplier or invoicing clients. Most times, a bank will require a different business account to give a business loan or credit extension.

2. *Employ a Bookkeeper or Get*
    Bookkeeping software

In the event that you sell something (product or service), you really want a stock inventory function in your bookkeeping software's to oversee and follow inventory. The product ought to have record and diary passages and the capacity to create financial statements.

There are numerous accounting and bookkeeping services that can do all of this for you, and that's only the tip of the iceberg. These services can be gotten online from any PC or phone and frequently incorporate elements like bank invoicing. Check out the best bookkeeping software's for Businesses or companies, or see whether you need to deal with the accounting yourself.

3. *Decide Your Make back the initial investment Point*

Before you fund your business, you should find out about your startup costs. To decide these, make a rundown of the number of physical supplies you really want, estimate the expense of any expert services you will require, decide the cost of any licenses or permits expected to work and compute the cost of office space or other real estate. Include the expenses of finance and payroll, if applicable.

Organizations can require a very long time to make profit, so it's smarter to overestimate the startup costs and have an excess of cash than pretty much nothing. Numerous specialists recommend having sufficient money available to cover a half year of working costs.

At the point when you know the amount you want to get everything rolling with your business, you really need to know the point where your business brings in cash. This figure is your break even from the original investment point..

Break point = Fixed cost ÷ Contribution margin

In contrast, the contribution margin = total number of sales revenue – cost to make the product

Chapter 6

Fund Your Business

There are various ways of funding your business — some require significant efforts while others are easier to acquire. **Two classes of financing exist: internal and external**

Internal financing

- ✓ *Individual reserve funds*
- ✓ *Funds from family and friends*
- ✓ *Credit cards*

In the event that you finance the business with your own assets or with credit cards, you need to pay the debt on the cards and you've lost a lump of your money if the business falls flat. By permitting your relatives or friends to put resources into your business, you are gambling bad sentiments and stressed connections assuming that the organization goes under. External funding is something that business owners who want to reduce these risks might consider

External funding incorporates:

- ✓ *Private or small business loans and credits*
- ✓ *Small business grants awards*

✓ *Private supporters funding/Crowd funding*

Although small businesses might need to use a blend of a few sources of capital. Consider how much cash is required, how long it will require before the Business can repay it and how risk-tolerant you are. Plan to make money, no matter which source you use. It's much better to bring back home six figures than make seven figures and just keep $80,000 of it.

Financing ideas include:

A. *Invoice factoring: through invoice factoring, you can offer unpaid invoices to another person at a discount. Business credit: Apply for a business line of credit, which is like an individual line of credit. As far as possible, loan cost will be based on your credit score, business' income, and financial history.*

B. *Equipment funding: In the event that you want to buy costly hardware for your business, you can finance it with a credit or lease. Microloans from the Small Business Administration (SBA) are loans of up to $50,000 that can be used for working capital, supplies or inventory, and machinery or equipment.*

C. *Grants and Awards: The federal government offers awards for Businesses, companies or organizations that advance development, export growth and development or are situated in historically disadvantaged regions. You can likewise grant through local and provincial organizations.*

D. *Crowdfunding: With crowdfunding, you can solicit donations from a large number of people or sell equity in your business to raise funds. Pick the right source of financial support for your business by considering how much cash you want, the time span for repayment and your capacity to bear risk.*

Request for Business Insurance

You really need to have insurance for your business, regardless of whether it's a locally situated business or even if you don't have any workers. The sort of insurance you really need relies upon your plan of action and what risk you face. You could require more than one type of policy, and you could require extra coverage as your business develops. In many states, workers' pay insurance is legally necessary on the off chance that you have workers.

Work with Agents to Get Insure

An insurance agent can help you find policies from insurers that offer the best rates and determine which coverages are appropriate for your business. A free insurance specialist or agent addresses a few unique safety net providers, so they can search for the best rates and coverage choices.

Essential Types of Business Insurance coverage.

Liability insurance safeguards your business against outsider cases of body injury, property damage and individual injury like slander or false advertising.

Property insurance covers the physical resources of your business, including your office space, tools and equipment.

Business interference insurance pays for the loss of income on the off chance that your business is compelled to close briefly because of a covered event like a cataclysmic event.

Products responsibility insurance safeguards against claims that your items caused discrimination injury or property harm.

Workers compensation insurance covers claims from workers charging segregation, inappropriate behavior or other unjust ends. Workers compensation insurance covers clinical costs and pay replacement for workers who are harmed during the Job.

Chapter 7

Get the Right Business Tools

Business Tools can assist with making your life simpler and make your business run all the more easily. You can save time, automate tasks, and make better decisions with the right tools.

Think about the resources you have at your disposal:

1. Accounting Software: lets you keep track of your company's income and expenses, make financial statements, and file taxes. E.g., QuickBooks and FreshBooks.

2. Software for customer relationship management (CRM): This will assist you in managing your relationships with customers, keeping track of data related to sales and marketing, and automating processes like customer service and follow-ups. Monday.com and Zoho CRM are two examples.

3. Software for project management lets you plan, carry out, and track projects. It can likewise be used to oversee worker assignments and allot assets. E.g. Airtable and ClickUp.

4. Credit card processor: This will permit you to accept credit card payments from clients. Examples include Stripe and PayPal.

5. Point of Sale (POS): A system that permits you to process client payments.

A few bookkeeping softwares and CRM softwares have POS features worked in. For example Clover and Lightspeed.

6. Virtual Private Network (VPN): Gives a protected, confidential association between your PC and the internet. This is significant for organizations' that handle sensitive information. NordVPN and ExpressVPN are great examples.

7. Merchants Services: When clients buy something, the cash is kept into your business account. You can likewise use this service to set up repeating charging or subscription payment. E.g. Square and Stripe.

8. Email hosting: This permits you to make an expert email address with your own domain name. E.g. incorporate G Suite and Microsoft Office365.

Build Your Business

By the time their products are launched, many business owners do not have enough money set aside for marketing. On the other hand, they've invested such a lot of energy creating the item that marketing is an afterthought.

> ➢ Make a Website

Regardless of whether you're a physical business, a website is fundamental. Making a site doesn't take long, either — you can have one done in as little as the end of the week. You can make a standard instructive site or an internet business webpage where you sell items online. In the event that you sell goods, services or products offline, include a portion in a web page for where clients can track down your location and hours.

> ➤ Make your website for SEO.

Subsequent to getting a site or e-commerce business store, centre on optimizing it for search engines (SEO). This way, the search engine can direct potential customers to your website when they search for specific keywords related to your products. SEO is a long term thing or procedure, so don't expect a lot of traffic from search engines at first — regardless of whether you're using the appropriate keywords.

> *Create Significant, Relevant and*
> *Quality Contents*

Give quality advanced content on your site that makes it simple for clients to find the right responses to their inquiries. Content promoting ideas incorporate other client's testimonials, blog posts, and Videos. Consider content promoting perhaps the most basic assignment on your day to day plan for every day. This is used related to posting via social media platforms like Instagram, Twitter (X), Facebook, and Ticktok.

> *Get Recorded in Web-based*
> *Catalogues (online directories)*

Clients use online registries like Google My Business, Yelp, and Facebook to track down nearby businesses. A few city offices of trade have professional business directories as well. Make sure your company is listed in as many relevant directories as you can. You can likewise make postings for your business on unambiguous registries that focus on your industry.

➢ *Create a Social Media Strategy:*

You need to be on social media as well because your potential customers use it every day. Post content that is intriguing and applicable to your target audience or market. Use Social Media to drive traffic back to your site where clients can become familiar with what you do and purchase your goods, products or services.

You don't have to be on each and every Social Media platform (although I'd recommend that) Nonetheless, you ought to have a presence on Facebook and Instagram in light of the fact that they offer e-commerce features that permit you to sell straightforwardly from your accounts. Both of these platforms have free training to assist you with advertising your business.

Chapter 8

Scale Your Business

To scale your business, you really need to develop your revenue. This can be accomplished by expanding your marketing efforts, , collaborating with other creators, improving the quality of your products and services, or adding new products or services that are in addition to what you already provide.

Ponder on ways you can mechanize or re-appropriate specific tasks so you can zero in on scaling the business. For instance, in the event that Social Media advertising and marketing is taking up a lot of your time, consider using a good site, for example, Hootsuite to assist you with dealing with your account more efficiently that way you'll save time.

You can likewise use innovation to mechanize specific business processes, including bookkeeping and lead generation. Doing this will give you additional opportunity to zero in on different parts of your business. It is essential to monitor your finances and ensure that your business is still profitable when scaling up. On the off chance that you're not making sufficient and enough money to take care of your expenses, you really want to either lessen your costs or increase your ways of expanding your income.

Construct and Build a Team

As your business develops, you'll have to designate tasks and create a good team of individuals who can assist you with running the everyday tasks. This could incorporate employing extra staff, workers for hire or even freelancers.

Assets for building a group include:

Platforms for hiring: Platforms for hiring, like Indeed and Glassdoor, can help you post job descriptions, review resumes, and conduct video interviews to find the best candidates.
Worksheets and Job boards; Job boards, for example, Craigslist and

*indeed permit you to post open
positions for nothing.
Social media: You can also find
potential employees by using social
media sites like Facebook and LinkedIn.
Freelance sites: using Upwork, and
Fiverr can assist you with finding
skilled specialists for one-time or long-
run jobs. You can likewise consider
specific errands, for example, customer
care, online entertainment advertising
or accounting. You could likewise
consider collaborating with different
businesses in your industry. For
instance, on the off chance that you're a
wedding organizer, you could
cooperate with an event planner,
photographic artist, etc. Along these
lines, you can offer your clients an all-
inclusive resource for all their wedding
needs.*

Another model is an e-commerce store that partners with a fulfilment centre. This sort of association can assist you with getting a good deal on delivery and storage expenses, and it can likewise assist you with getting your goods to your clients quicker.

To find partnership, look for Businesses in your industry that endorse or complement what you do. For instance, on the off chance that you're a website specialist, you could cooperate with a digital marketing organization. You can likewise look for organizations' that serve a similar objective market as you yet offer different products or services. For instance, on the off chance that you sell ladies' clothing, you could cooperate with a gems store (jewelry) or a hair salon.